Mastering Python Lists

Marc Poulin

Copyright 2015, Marc Poulin

Contents

1 Introduction   7
    Hello World! 7
    Trailing Commas 8

2 Empty Lists   9
    The [ ] Operator 9
    The List() Function 9
    Creating A Literal List Of Empty Lists 9
    Creating A List Of Empty Lists With A List Comprehension 10
    Avoid Using The Repeat Operator 11

3 Converting To Other Types   13
    Converting To A Set 13
    Converting To A Dictionary 14

4 Unpacking a List   15
    Unpacking In Python 3.X 15
    Unpacking A List Into Function Arguments 17

5 Iterating Over a List   19
    Iterable Objects 19
    Iterating Over All Items 20
    The For Statement 20
    The Enumerate Function 20

6 Copying a List   23
    List Variables 23
    The List() Function 24
    The Copy() Function 24
    Slicing 24

7 Subscripts — 25
Negative Subscripts — 25
Conversion Formulas — 26

8 Ranges — 27
Parameters — 27
Examples — 28

9 Range Slices — 29
Default Values — 29
Forward Range Slices — 30
    With Positive Parameters — 30
    Summary — 31
    With Negative Parameters — 31
    Summary — 32
Reverse Range Slices — 32
    With Positive Parameters — 32
    Summary — 33
    With Negative Parameters — 33
    Summary — 34

10 List Slices — 35
Slice Syntax — 35
Quick Copy — 35
Quick Reversed Copy — 36

11 Forward List Slices — 39
Default Values — 40
Skipping Items — 41

12 Reverse List Slices — 43
Default Values — 43

13 List Comprehensions — 45
Example 1 — 45
Example 2 — 46
Differences Between Python 2.x And 3.x — 46

14 Boolean Operations — 47
Equality and Identity — 47
If and While Statements — 48
The Any() and All() Functions — 48

15 Processing Multiple Lists — 51
- Processing Lists In Series — 51
- The Zip() Function — 51
- Unzipping — 53
- Transposing A Matrix — 53
- Tic Tac Toe — 54

16 Sorting — 57
- Sorting In Place — 57
- Creating A Sorted Copy — 57
- Reverse Sort — 57
- Specifying A Sort Key — 58
- Lambda Functions — 58

17 Adding Items To A List — 59
- Adding One Item To The End — 59
- Extending A List — 60
- Adding One Item In The Middle — 61
- Adding Multiple Items In The Middle — 62

18 Removing Items From a List — 63
- Removing An Item By Index — 63
- Removing One Or More Items By Value — 63

19 Reversing a List — 65
- Reverse Method — 65
- Reversed Function — 66

20 Removing Duplicate Values — 67
- Removing Duplicates Without Preserving Order — 67
- Removing Duplicates While Preserving Order — 67

21 Searching for Values — 69
- Testing For The Presence Of An Item — 69
- Finding The Index Of An Item — 69
- Finding The Indexes Of Duplicates — 70
- Finding The Largest Or Smallest Value — 70
- Finding The Index Of The Largest Or Smallest Value — 70

22 Counting Values — 71
- The Count() Method — 71
- The Counter Class — 71

Chapter 1

Introduction

Lists are a powerful feature of Python but most books only scratch the surface. They teach you the basic syntax (the "what") but leave out practical examples (the "why"). This book goes beyond basic syntax and tries to show you the real power of lists.

So why aren't lists more widely used?

When you first learn to program, the focus is on individual variables and objects. Lists require you to go beyond that way of thinking and see your data in "chunks" instead.

Many problems are best solved by manipulating lists of data. Python's list operators are a natural fit for these types of problems. They let you write solutions that are both compact and efficient. In short, by learning to "think in lists" you will become a better Python programmer.

Hello World!

It's customary to start a programming book with a simple "Hello World!" example, and who am I to break with tradition?

```
greeting = ['Hello', 'World']
```

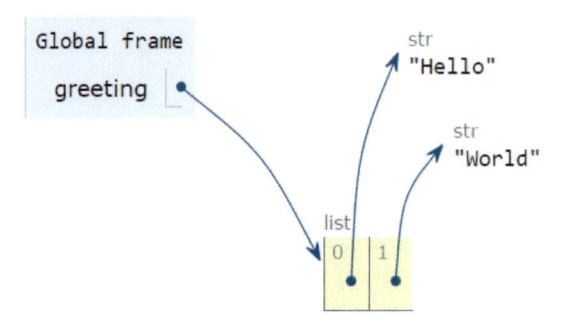

This is a "literal" definition of a list. It consists of a comma-separated series of values enclosed in square brackets.

This particular list contains two string values. Lists can contain any type of value, and different types can be mixed together in the same list.

List values can span multiple lines. Here is the same list formatted a bit differently.

```
greeting = [
    'Hello',
    'World'
]
```

Trailing Commas

The last item in a list can be followed by an optional "trailing comma". This comma has no effect, but Python allows it so you don't have to treat the last value differently from the others.

```
greeting = [
    'Hello',
    'World', # trailing comma
]
```

Chapter 2

Empty Lists

You might want to create empty lists and fill in the values at a later time.

The [ ] Operator

The easiest way to create an empty list is with the list operator [ ].

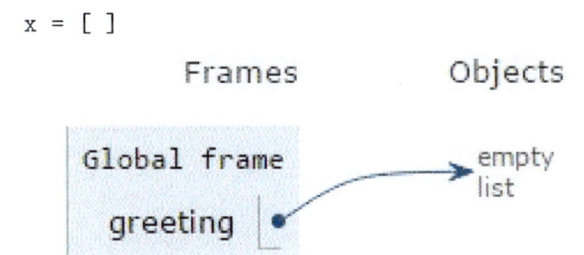

```
x = [ ]
```

The List() Function

Another way to create an empty list is by calling the list() function with no parameters. The function will return an empty list

```
x = list()
```

Creating A Literal List Of Empty Lists

Now we discuss creating a list of empty lists (empty sub-lists). If the number of sub-list is small, you can specify them literally.

```
x = [ [], [], [], ]
```

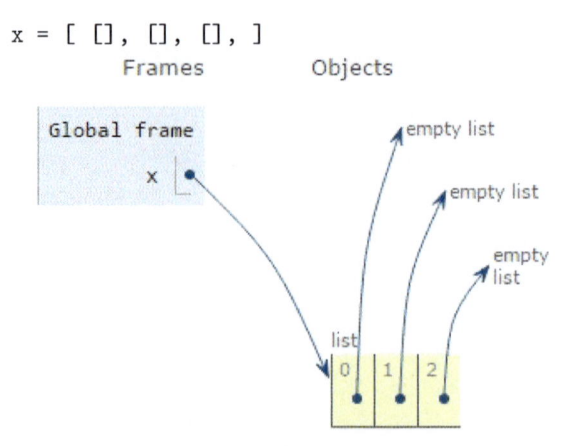

Creating A List Of Empty Lists With A List Comprehension

If the number of sub-lists is large, you can use a list comprehension to generate the list. This reduces the amount of typing you need to do.

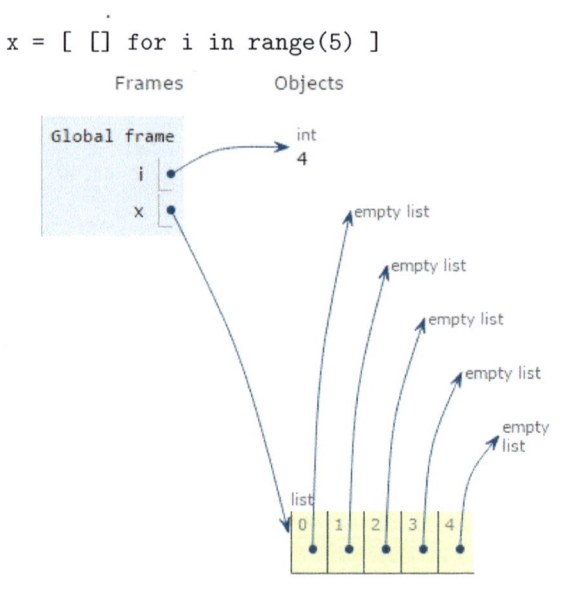

```
x = [ [] for i in range(5) ]
```

You will learn more about list comprehensions in Chapter 13.

Avoid Using The Repeat Operator

Lists, like other sequence types, support the repeat operator *. It may be tempting to use the repeat operator to generate a list of empty lists.

Be careful! This will NOT create distinct sub-lists. Instead, it will create ONE sub-list and fill the main list with multiple references to that ONE list.

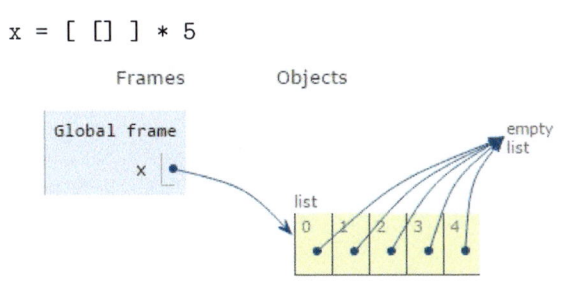

```
x = [ [] ] * 5
```

Stop and compare this diagram to the one on the previous page.

Chapter 3

Converting To Other Types

Converting To A Set

A new set object can be produced from a list by passing the list to the set() function.

Duplicate values are eliminated, so

```
set([1,1,1])
```

produces

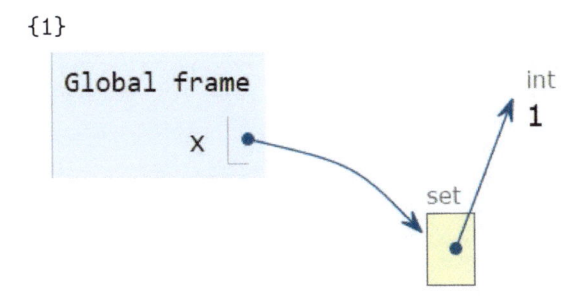

{1}

```
Global frame
    x
set
int
1
```

Order is not preserved, so

```
set([1,2,3,1,1])
```

might produce

{1,2,3}, {1,3,2}, or {2,3,1}

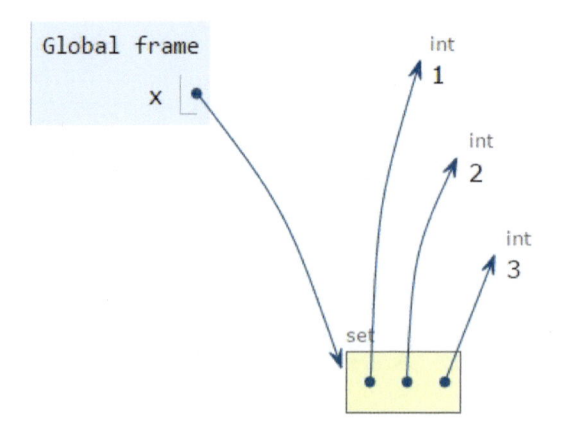

Converting To A Dictionary

A new dictionary can be produced from a list of (key, value) pairs by passing the list to the dict() function.

    dict([('a',1),('b',2),('c',3)])

will produce

    {'a':1, 'b':2, 'c':3}.

Chapter 4

Unpacking a List

A list can be unpacked into separate variables. This is done with a multiple assignment statement.

```
x = [1,2,3]
a, b, c = x
```

Unpacking In Python 3.X

In Python 2.x, the number of variables must exactly match the number of values to unpack. Python 3.x relaxes this restriction by adding a starred variable syntax, where the starred variable will contain a (possibly empty) list of values.

Note: The starred variable is used only if the number of list items exceeds the number of unstarred variables.

Note: there can only be one starred variable in the assignment list.

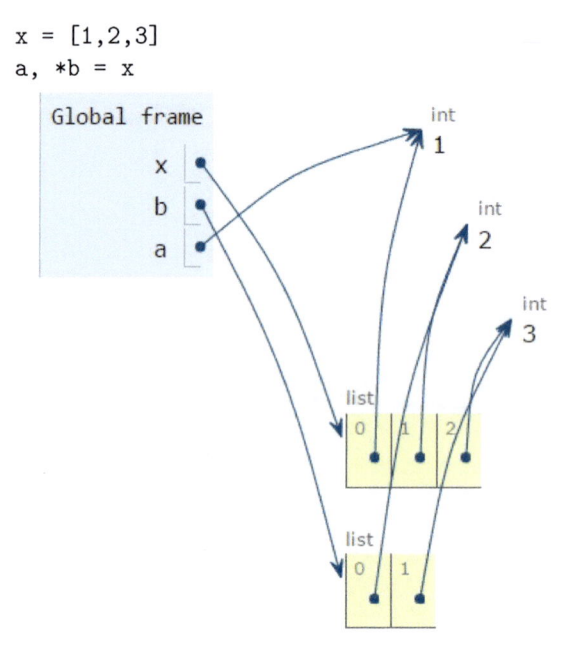

```
x = [1,2,3]
a, *b = x
```

Here there are enough unstarred variables to account for all the values, so the starred variable contains an empty list.

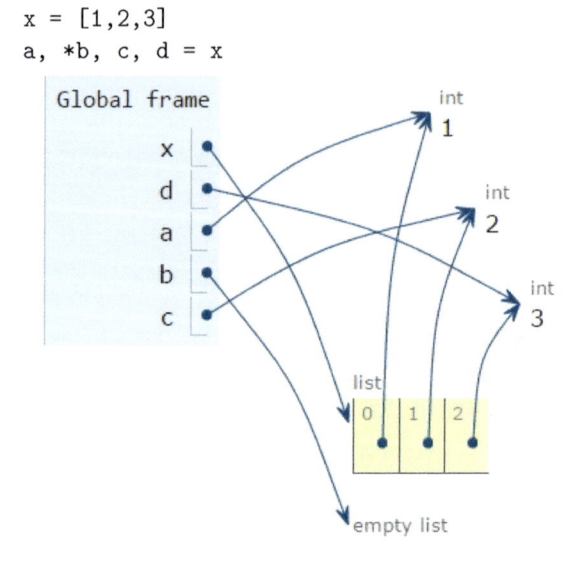

```
x = [1,2,3]
a, *b, c, d = x
```

Unpacking A List Into Function Arguments

A list can also be unpacked into function arguments with the "*" operator.

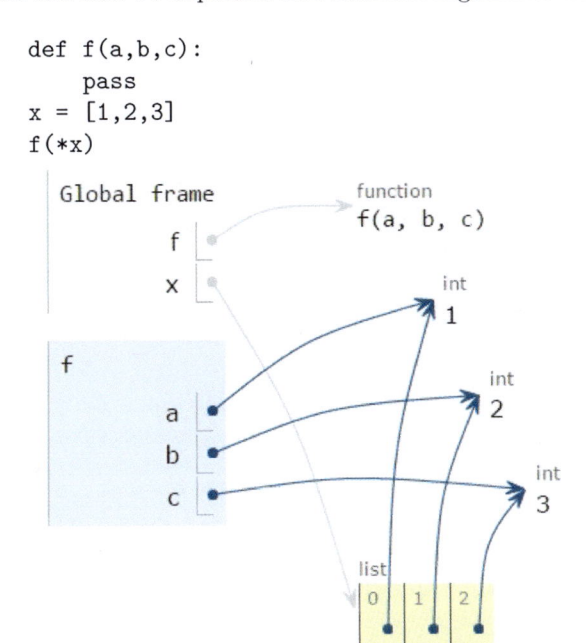

```
def f(a,b,c):
    pass
x = [1,2,3]
f(*x)
```

Chapter 5

Iterating Over a List

Iterable Objects

Iteration allows you to retrieve the values from a list one at a time. List are iterable, which means they implement Python's iteration protocol. The iteration protocol is based on iterator objects.

Given a list

```
x = [1,2,3]
```

You can call the __iter__() method to get an iterator for the list

```
it = x.__iter__()
```

The iterator object has a __next__() method, which returns each item in the list one by one.

What happens when there are no more items? The iterator object raises a StopIteration exception to let you know you have reached the end of the sequence.

This is what it looks like in the interactive Python shell:

```
>>> x = [1,2,3]
>>> it = x.__iter__()
>>> it.__next__() 1
>>> it.__next__() 2
>>> it.__next__() 3
>>> it.__next__()
Traceback (most recent call last):
    File "<stdin>", line 1, in <module>StopIteration
>>>
```

Iterating Over All Items

If you wanted to print all the items in a list, you could use a counter variable to keep track of how many times you should call __next__().

```
x = [1,2,3]
it = x.__iter__()
count = 0
while count < len(x):
    item = it.__next__())
    print(item)
    count = count + 1
```

This is how you would loop over a list in other languages like C or Java. Fortunately, Python provides a simpler alternative.

The For Statement

Using raw iterators is very cumbersome and error prone. Python provides a for statement which takes care of all the details of creating the iterator, calling __next__ (), and testing for *StopIteration*.

Here is the same code using a for loop. The for statement implicitly sets *item* to the next value in *x*.

```
x = [1,2,3]
for item in x:
    print(item)
```

WARNING: Do not re-size a list (add or remove items) while you are iterating over it. The iterator keeps an internal count of how many times __next__() has been called and resizing the list will invalidate this count.

The Enumerate Function

The enumerate function can be used to number items in a list. Numbering starts at 0 by default. This can be useful in cases where you need to know each item's index number. The return value is a list containing (number, item) pairs.

Given

```
x = ['a', 'b', 'c']
```

enumerate(x) produces a list of tuples. Each tuple contains a count and a value.

THE ENUMERATE FUNCTION

```
[(0,'a'), (1,'b'), (2,'c')]
```

Do you need to know the index value of each item? You can call the enumerate() function in a for statement instead of using a counter variable.

```
for e in enumerate(x):
    index = e[0]
    value = e[1]
    print(index, value)
```

Unpacking also works in a for statement, so you can unpack the tuples directly into variables. That's usually more convenient.

```
for index, value in enumerate(x):
    print(index, value)
```

Chapter 6

Copying a List

List Variables

Python has an assignment operator but it works a bit differently from other languages. *Assigning one variable to another does not copy the object.* It just creates another name for the same object.

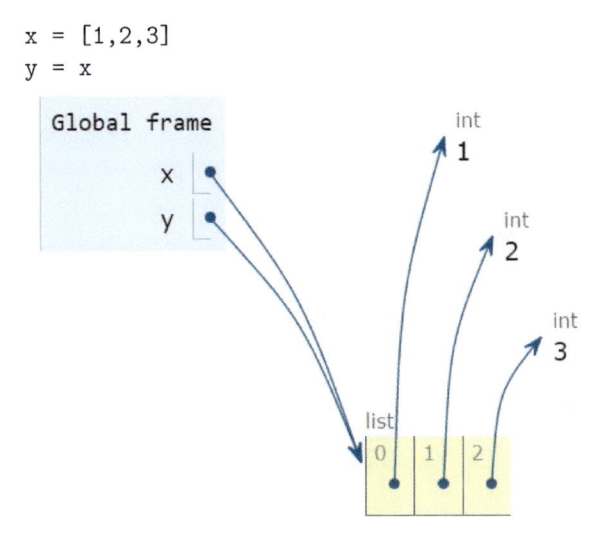

```
x = [1,2,3]
y = x
```

Notice that the variables x and y both refer to the exact same list. It's important for you to understand this, because any changes you make to x will be visible in y. If you want a new object, you must explicitly create it.

The List() Function

The built in list() function will create a new list from any iterable object. Since lists are iterable objects, you can use list() to make a copy.

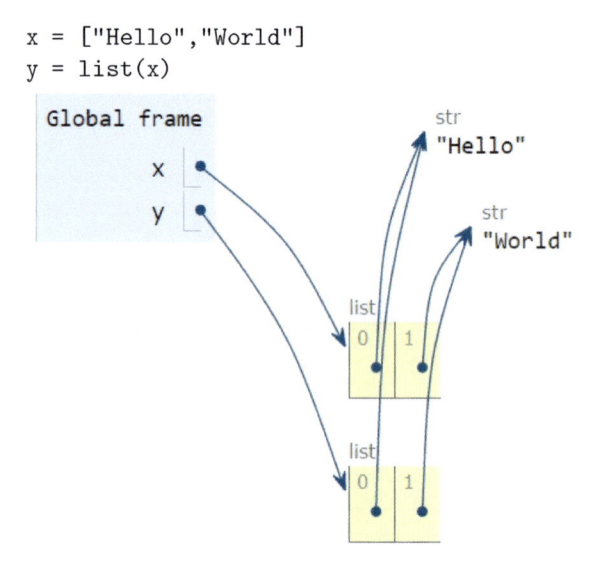

```
x = ["Hello","World"]
y = list(x)
```

Although we speak of lists "containing" values, this is not strictly true. Lists contain "references" to objects, not the objects themselves. *When you copy a list it is the references that are copied, not the objects.* Notice in this example there are still only two string objects, not four.

The Copy() Function

You can import the copy() from the copy module and use it to copy a list. This is a general-purpose function that be used to copy any object.

```
from copy import copy
x = [1,2,3]
y = copy(x)
```

Slicing

Slicing a list is a third way of making a copy. You will learn all about slices in later chapters.

Chapter 7

Subscripts

Each list item occupies a specific position. Positions are numbered starting at 0 and each item can be referenced by it's position number (called the "index"). You subscript a list object by specifying the index number in square brackets.

> `list_object[index]`

Negative Subscripts

For convenience, Python allows both positive and negative subscripts. Normal Python subscripts (like subscripts in most other languages) start at 0 and are relative to the start of the list.

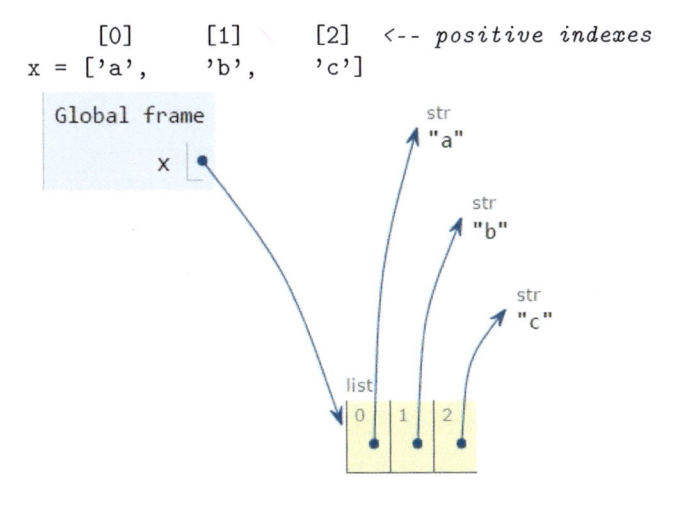

```
        [0]     [1]     [2]    <-- positive indexes
x = ['a',      'b',     'c']
```

But subscripts can also be specified from the end of the list using negative indexes.

```
        [0]    [1]    [2]   <-- positive indexes
x = ['a',   'b',   'c']
        [-3]   [-2]   [-1]  <-- negative indexes
```

This means the first item can always be accessed as x[0] and the last item can always be accessed as x[-1], even without knowing the length of the list.

```
first = x[0]
last = x[-1]
```

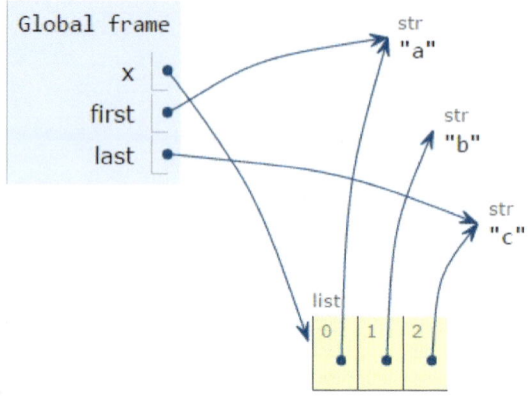

Alternatively (and in other languages that don't support negative subscripts) you could compute the last index as

```
x[len(x)-1]
```

This is slower (requiring a function call), longer to type, harder to read, and more prone to errors.

Conversion Formulas

You can easily convert between positive and negative subscripts if you know the length of the list.

Let P be the positive index, N be the negative index, and L be the list length. Then

```
P = L + N    # converting a known negative to a positive
```

and

```
N = P - L    # converting a known positive to a negative
```

Chapter 8

Ranges

In Python 2.x, the range() and xrange() functions can be used to produce a list of numbers in either ascending or descending order.

NOTE: in Python 3.x, the xrange() function has been renamed to range().

Parameters

The range(start, stop, step) function takes 3 parameters.

start the first number of the range (optional, defaults to 0)

stop the last number of the range (not included in the result)

step controls ascending/descending and the interval between numbers (optional, defaults to +1). The step can be positive or negative. If step > 0, numbers are produced by counting UP from start to stop (not including stop). If step < 0, numbers are produced by counting DOWN from start to stop (not including stop). The step can also skip over values. If step = 2, the output contains every 2nd value, if step = 3, the output contains every 3rd value, etc.

The xrange (Python 2.x) and range (Python 3.x) functions return iterator objects. Use the list() function to turn the iteration into an actual list.

```
x = list(xrange(5))
```

Examples

Range	Produces
range(10)	[0, 1, 2, 3, 4, 5, 6, 7, 8, 9] - start defaults to 0
range(5, 10)	[5, 6, 7, 8, 9]
range(10 ,0)	[] - there is no way to get from 10 to 0 by counting UP
range(10, 0, -1)	[10, 9, 8, 7, 6, 5, 4, 3, 2, 1]
range(10, 0, -2)	[10, 8, 6, 4, 2] - range counts down by 2's

REMEMBER: the stop value is always excluded from the output

Chapter 9

Range Slices

Range slices are new feature of Python 3.x. Understanding range slices will prepare us to look at list slices in Lesson 14.

    `range_object`[start : end : stride]

The slice syntax is similar to the subscripting syntax (they both use square brackets). A slice is specified with 3 parameters, all of which are optional. The parameters are separated by a ":" character.

start the start of the range to copy

end the end of the range to copy.

stride the direction in which copying takes place and the number of items to skip over.

REMEMBER: the end value is always excluded from the result.

Default Values

The start, end, and stride parameters all have default values.

start defaults to the first item in the list

end defaults to everything after the start (including the last item)

stride defaults to 1

Forward Range Slices

Slicing a range object produces another range object. This second range object will generate the desired values.

By examining these slice objects in the Python shell you can see how the start, end, and stride values are being interpreted.

With Positive Parameters

Positive start and end values are relative to the beginning of the range.

The full range

```
>>> x = range(5)
>>> x
range(0, 5)
>>> list(x)
[0, 1, 2, 3, 4]
```

All values from the first to the last

```
>>> x[::]
range(0, 5)
>>> list(x[::])
[0, 1, 2, 3, 4]
```

All values from x[2] to the last

```
>>> x[2::]
range(2, 5)
>>> list(x[2::])
[2, 3, 4]
```

All values from x[2] up to but not including x[4]

```
>>> x[2:4]
range(2, 4)
>>> list(x[2:4:])
[2, 3]
```

All values from x[1] to the last, skipping every other value

```
>>> x[1::2]
range(1, 5, 2)
>>> list(x[1::2])
[1, 3]
```

FORWARD RANGE SLICES

Summary

Slice	Equivalent Range	Produces	Description
x[::]	range(0, 5)	[0, 1, 2, 3, 4]	All values from the first to the last
x[2::]	range(2, 5)	[2, 3, 4]	All values from x[2] to the last
x[2:4]	range(2, 4)	[2, 3]	All values from x[2] up to but not including x[4]
x[1::2]	range(1, 5, 2)	[1, 3]	All values from x[1] to the last, skipping every other value

With Negative Parameters

Earlier, you saw how negative list indexes are relative to the end of the list. Similarly, negative start and end values are relative to the end of the range.

Spend some time studying these examples to make sure you really understand what's going on. Notice how Python converts negative values to their positive equivalents.

The full range

```
>>> x = range(5)
>>> x range(0, 5)
>>> list(x)
[0, 1, 2, 3, 4]
```

All the values from x[-2] to the last

```
>>> x[-2::]
range(3, 5)
>>> list(x[-2::])
[3, 4]
```

The values from x[-2] up to but not including x[-1]

```
>>> x[-2:-1:]
range(3, 4)
>>> list(x[-2:-1:])
[3]
```

All the values from x[-4] to the last, skipping every other value

```
>>> x[-4::2]
range(1, 5, 2)
>>> list(x[-4::2])
[1, 3]
```

Summary

Slice	Equivalent Range	Produces	Description
x[-2::]	range(3, 5)	[3, 4]	All the values from x[-2] to the last
x[-2:-1:]	range(3, 4)	[3]	The values from x[-2] up to but not including x[-1]
x[-4::2]	range(1, 5, 2)	[1, 3]	All the values from x[-4] to the last, skipping every other value

Reverse Range Slices

A negative step value will produce a reverse slice. In a reverse slice, the values are produced by counting down from the start to the end.

With Positive Parameters

Positive start and end values are relative to the beginning of the range.

The full range

```
>>> x = range(5)
>>> x
range(0, 5)
>>> list(x)
[0, 1, 2, 3, 4]
```

All values from the last to the first

```
>>> x[::-1]
range(4, -1, -1)
>>> list(x[::-1])
[4, 3, 2, 1, 0]
```

All values from x[2] to the first

REVERSE RANGE SLICES

```
>>> x[2::-1]
range(2, -1, -1)
>>> list(x[2::-1])
[2, 1, 0]
```

All values from x[4] down to but not including x[2]

```
>>> x[4:2:-1]
range(4, 2, -1)
>>> list(x[4:2:-1])
[4, 3]
```

All values from x[4] to the first, skipping every other value

```
>>> x[4::-2]
range(4, -1, -2)
>>> list(x[4::-2])
[4, 2, 0]
```

Summary

Slice	Equivalent Range	Produces	Description
x[::-1]	range(4, -1, -1)	[4, 3, 2, 1, 0]	All values from the last to the first
x[2::-1]	range(2, -1, -1)	[2, 1, 0]	All values from x[2] to the first
x[4:2:-1]	range(4, 2, -1)	[4, 3]	All values from x[4] down to but not including x[2]
x[4::-2]	range(4, -1, -2)	[4, 2, 0]	All values from x[4] to the first, skipping every other value

With Negative Parameters

Negative start and end values are relative to the end of the range.
The full range

```
>>> x = range(5)
>>> x
range(0, 5)
>>> list(x)
[0, 1, 2, 3, 4]
```

All the values from x[-2] down to the first

```
>>> x[-2::-1]
range(3, -1, -1)
>>> list(x[-2::-1])
[3, 2, 1, 0]
```

The values from x[-1] down to but not including x[-2]

```
>>> x[-1:-2:-1]
range(4, 3, -1)
>>> list(x[-1:-2:-1])
[4]
```

All the values from x[-4] down to the first, skipping every other value

```
>>> x[-1::-2]
range(4, -1, -2)
>>> list(x[-1::-2])
[4, 2, 0]
```

Summary

Slice	Equivalent Range	Produces	Description
x[-2::-1]	range(3, -1, -1)	[3, 2, 1, 0]	All the values from x[-2] down to the first
x[-1:-2:-1]	range(4, 3, -1)	[4]	The values from x[-1] down to but not including x[-2]
x[-1::-2]	range(4, -1, -2)	[4, 2, 0]	All the values from x[-4] down to the first, skipping every other value

Chapter 10

List Slices

Now that we've looked at range slices, we are ready to talk about list slices.

The slice operator specifies a range of list indexes. Items from this range are copied from the original list into a new list object. Although this lesson is about lists, you should know that slicing can also be applied to strings, tuples, and Python 3.x ranges.

Slice Syntax

`list_object`[start : end : stride]

The slice syntax is similar to the subscripting syntax (they both use square brackets). A slice is specified with 3 parameters, all of which are optional. The parameters are separated by a ":" character.

start the start of the range to copy

end the end of the range to copy

stride the direction in which copying takes place and the number of items to skip over

REMEMBER: the end value is always excluded from the result

Quick Copy

Using the default values for start, end, and stride will copy every item in the list. This is a quick alternative to using either the copy() or list() functions.

```
x = [1,2]
y = x[::]
```

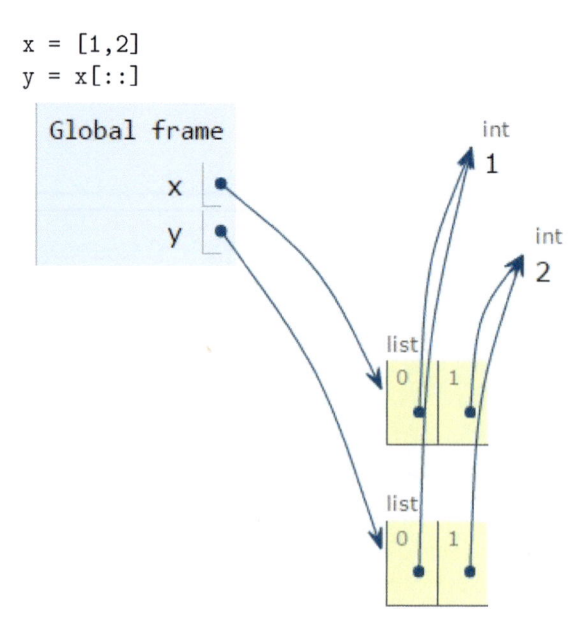

[Diagram: Global frame with x and y both pointing to separate list objects, each containing references to int 1 and int 2]

Quick Reversed Copy

Using a stride of -1 with default start and end values will produce a reversed copy.

```
x = [1,2]
y = x[::-1]
```

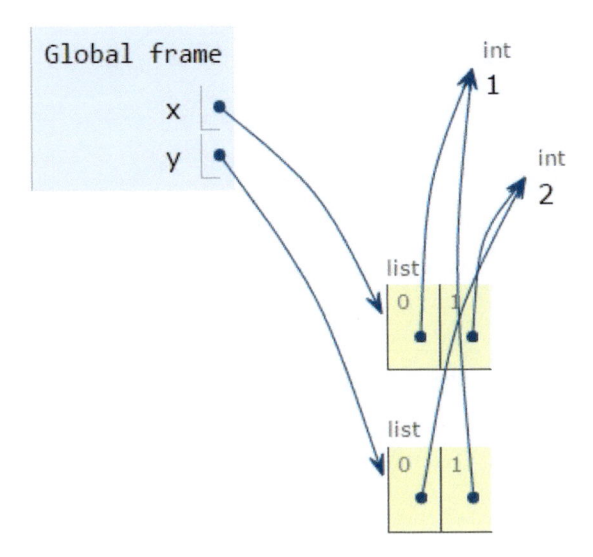

Chapter 11

Forward List Slices

Using a stride > 0 (or letting the stride value default) will produce a forward slice. A forward slice copies everything from the start index up to (but not including) the end index.

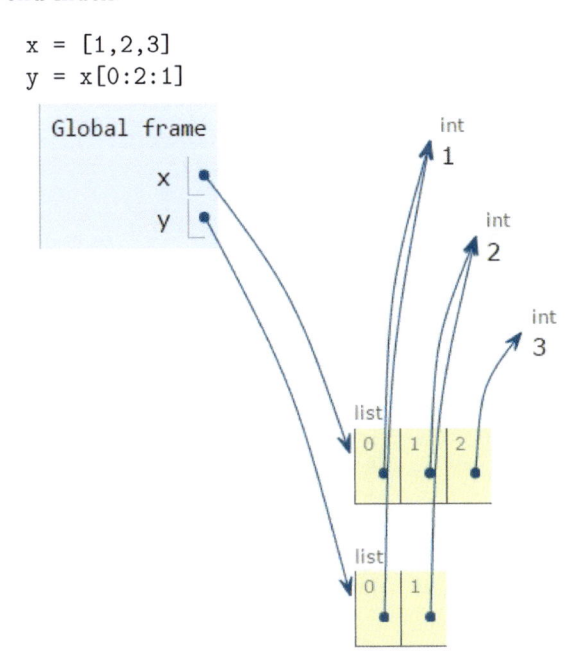

```
x = [1,2,3]
y = x[0:2:1]
```

NOTE: x[2] is not copied into y because we gave an explict end value.

If you want the last value to be included in the slice, either let the end value default or set it to *len(x)*.

```
x = [1,2,3]
y = x[0:len(x):1]
z = x[0::1]
```

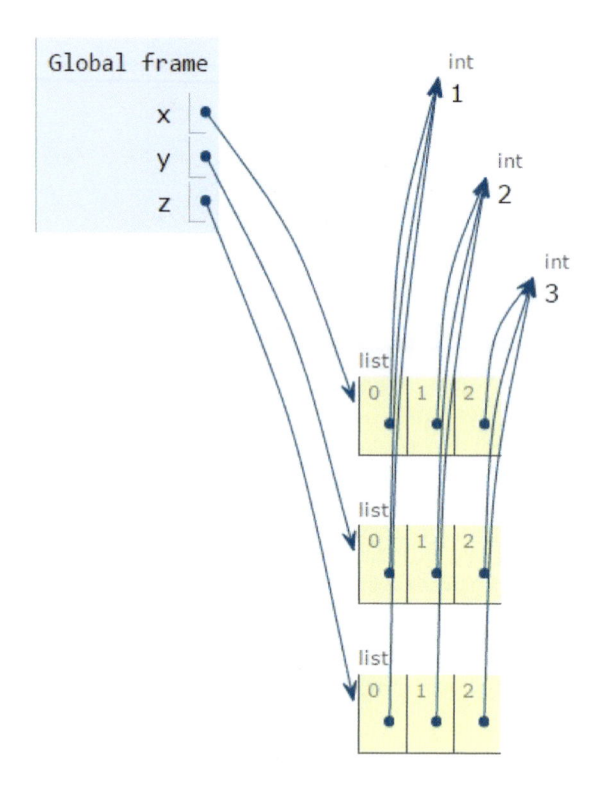

Default Values

The start, end, and stride parameters have default values.

start defaults to the first item in the list

end defaults to everything after the start (including the last item)

stride defaults to 1

Note that a default end value [::1] is not the same as specifying the last item [:-1:1]. In the first case ([::1]) the last item is include in the slice, while in the second case ([:-1:1]) it is not.

Skipping Items

Using a stride > 1 will skip values. A stride of 2 will copy every 2nd value, a stride of 3 will copy every 3rd value, and so forth.

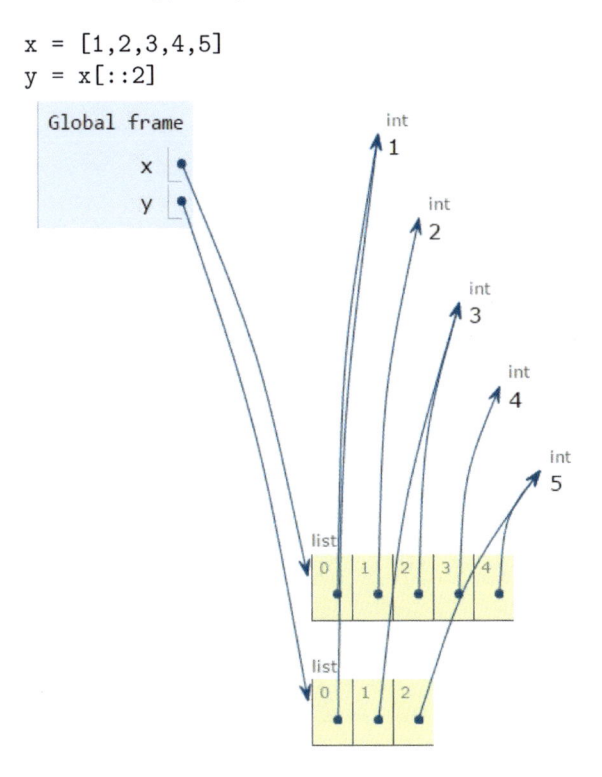

```
x = [1,2,3,4,5]
y = x[::2]
```

Chapter 12

Reverse List Slices

Specifying a stride < 0 will produce a reverse slice. Items are copied *backwards* from the start down to (but not including) the end.

Default Values

The start and end parameters both have default values.

start defaults to the last item of the list.

end defaults to everything ahead of the start (including the first item)

There is no default stride. If you want a reverse slice you must specify a negative stride explicitly.

REMEMBER: using a default end value is not the same as specifying an end value of 0. In the first case ([-1::-1]) item [0] is included in the slice, while in the second case ([-1:0:-1]) it is not.

Chapter 13

List Comprehensions

List comprehensions combine list syntax, for statement syntax, and if statement syntax into one statement. They look complicated because they combine a lot of different syntax into one statement. But don't worry — everything you know about for and if statements still applies.

The syntax of a list comprehension consists of 3 parts enclosed in square brackets.

```
new_list_object = [output-expression for-clause if-clause]
```

It works by iterating over an input list (the FOR CLAUSE), testing the values (the IF CLAUSE), and computing an output value (the OUTPUT EXPRESSION). It is equivalent to

```
new_list_object = []
for i in source_list:
    if (if-clause(i)):
        new_list_object.append(output-expression(i))
```

Example 1

Given a list of numbers, produce a new list containing each number * 2 only if the original number is less than 3.

```
x = [1,2,3,4,5]
y = [i*2 for i in x if i<3]
```

Complex comprehensions can be split across multiple lines if it makes them easier to read.

```
y = [i*2
     for i in x
     if i<3]
```

But if the comprehension gets too complicated, it's best to use a regular for loop.

Example 2

Given a list of strings, how would you create a new list that contains (string, len(string)) tuples? Specifically, how would you transform ['Hello', 'World'] into [('Hello', 5), ('World', 5)]?

Here is a solution using an explicit for loop:

```
words = ['Hello', 'World']
output = []
for word in words:
    output.append((word, len(word)))
```

And here is the equivalent logic using a list comprehension

```
words = ['Hello', 'World']
output = [(word, len(word)) for word in words]
```

The comprehension takes care of creating a new list object and inserting the calculated values into the new list (without using the append method).

Differences Between Python 2.x And 3.x

Variables behave differently in Python 2.x and 3.x. In Python 2.x, any variables created inside the comprehension continue to exist outside the comprehension. In Python 3.x, variables inside the comprehension are private.

```
x = [1,2,3]
x_squares = [i*i for i in x]
```

In Python 3.x, any attempt to use i outside the comprehension will raise a *NameError* exception.

Chapter 14

Boolean Operations

Equality and Identity

Python provides two comparison operators: *is* and $==$
   x is y returns True if x and y both refer to the same object
   $x == y$ returns True if the values of x and y are equal

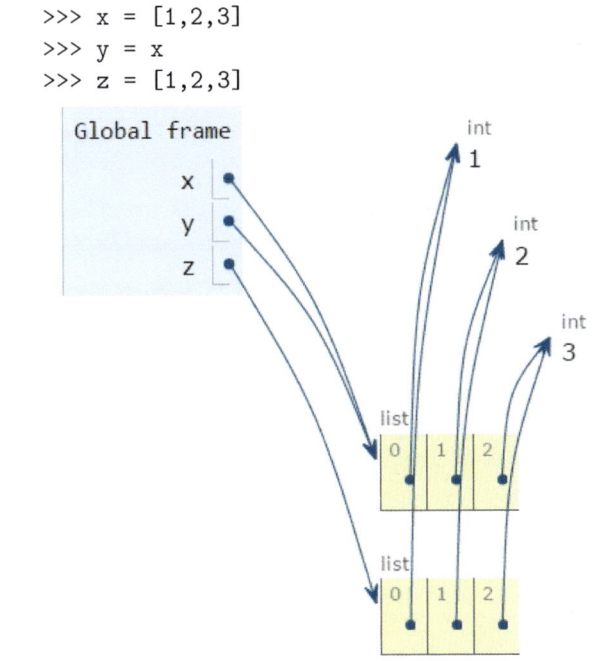

```
>>> x = [1,2,3]
>>> y = x
>>> z = [1,2,3]
```

```
>>> x is y
True
>>> x == y
True
>>> x is z
False
>>> x == z
True
```

If and While Statements

You often need to determine whether or not a list is empty. Since this is such a common situation, Python provides a simplified syntax for testing this. In an if or while statement, a list variable evaluates to False when the list is empty and True when it is not.

if len(x)>0: can be written *if x:*
while len(x)>0: can be written *while x:*

The Any() and All() Functions

These two built-in functions return a logical True or False based on the contents of a list.

The all() function performs a logical AND across all the items in list. It returns True if all the items evaluate to True.

The any() function performs a logical OR across all the items in a list. It returns True if at least one item evaluates to True.

You can use the logical not operator in combination with any() and all() to test for other variations.

all — True if every value is True

not any — True if every value is False

any — True if at least 1 value is True

not all — True if at least 1 value is False

The any() and all() functions can be nested to form AND/OR tables (decision tables). These can be used instead of if statements to encode complex business logic.

For example, consider what happens when you make a withdrawal from a bank account. The bank needs to look at your account balance, the withdrawal amount, and any overdraft line of credit that might be available.

```
    approved = any(
        all(balance >= amount),
        all(balance < amount, available_credit > amount)),
    )
    if approved:
        # process withdrawal
```

This is just a simple example. A real application might need to consider dozens of rules and complex relationships between them.

Chapter 15

Processing Multiple Lists

Processing Lists In Series

The obvious way to process lists sequentially is to concatenate them with the + operator. This has the effect of combining all the lists into a single list.

```
x = [1,2,3]
y = [4,5,6]
for i in x+y:
    print(i)
```

This will print 1 2 3 4 5 6

NOTE: Concatenation requires copying the lists. This can be inefficient if the lists are large. The itertools module provides a chain function. It has the same effect as the "+" operator but the lists are not copied.

```
import itertools
for i in itertools.chain(x,y):
    print(i)
```

The Zip() Function

The zip function combines multiple lists in parallel by collecting all the items at each position into a single tuple.

For example, if you have two lists

```
a = [1,2,3]
b = ['a','b','c']
```

The result of zip(a,b) would be

```
[ (a[0], b[0]), (a[1], b[1]), (a[2], b[2]), ]
```

This is useful if you want to iterate over multiple lists at the same time without using a counter variable.

Let's look at another example. Given a list of cities and a list of countries, how would you print each city/country pair?

```
cities = ['Madrid', 'Rome', 'Paris']
countries = ['Spain', 'Italy', 'France']
```

Without zip, you would need three things:

1. a counter variable to keep track of where you are in the iteration

2. a call to the range() function to generate the subscript values

3. a subscript on each list to retrieve the values

Your code might look like this

```
for i in range(len(cities)):
    city = cities[i]
    country = countries[i]
    print(city, country)
```

This might look familiar if you have experience in other programming languages. Using zip, your code would look like this

```
for city, country in zip(cities,countries):
    print(city, country)
```

How this works:

- zip produces a list of tuples

- the for statement iterates over the tuples

- each tuple is unpacked into the city and country variables

Unzipping

There is no unzip() function, but you can achieve the same result with the "*" operator.

Given

```
z = zip(a, b, c)
```

you can use

```
a, b, c = zip(*z)
```

to recover the original lists.

Transposing A Matrix

The zip function can also be used to extract individual columns from a matrix, or to transpose the entire matrix.

Given a 3x3 matrix

```
[ [1,2,3], [4,5,6], [7,8,9], ]
```

the transpose would be

```
[ [1,4,7], [2,5,8], [3,6,9], ]
```

The rows become columns and the columns become rows.

If you have a 2 dimensional matrix like

```
x = [ [1,2,3], [4,5,6], [7,8,9], ]
```

It's easy to access the rows. But how do you extract the columns? One way is with nested for loops

```
ROWS = len(x)
COLUMNS = len(x[0])
x_transpose = []
for column in range(COLUMNS):
    r = []
    for row in range(ROWS):
        r.append(x[row][column])
    x_transpose.append(r)
```

Another way is to flatten the matrix and slice out the columns (using stride to skip to the next row).

```
x_transpose = []
values = []
for row in x:
    values.extend(row)
# values contains [1,2,3,4,5,6,7,8,9]
for column in COLUMNS:
    x_transpose.append(x[column::COLUMNS])
```

But the easiest way is to use zip.

```
x_transpose = zip(*x)
```

The secret is the "*" operator, which unpacks the matrix and passes the individual rows to zip.

zip(*x) is equivalent to *zip(x[0], x[1], x[2])*
which is equivalent to *zip([1,2,3], [4,5,6], [7,8,9])*
which returns *[(1,4,7), (2,5,8), (3,6,9)]*

Tic Tac Toe

I assume you are familiar with the game *tic-tac-toe*. If you are programming this game, one problem you need to solve is how to check for a winner. Here is one approach. Assume the board is a 3x3 matrix of X's and O's like

```
board = [
    ['x', '', 'x'],
    ['', 'o', ''],
    ['', 'o', '']
]
```

A player wins if any row, column, or diagonal contains all X's or all O's. Here's one possible implementation. The secret is in setting up a list containing all rows, columns, and diagonals. Then you can determine the winner with a single line of code.

```
def is_winner(player, board):
    '''
    Return true if player is a winner.
    Player can be "x" or "o".

    Iterate over all the rows, columns, and diagonals.
    Player wins if the player appears 3 times in
```

TIC TAC TOE

```
    any row, column, or diagonal.
    '''

    assert player in 'xo'    # check player

    rows = board
    assert len(rows) == 3

    columns = zip(*board)
    assert len(columns) == 3

    diagonals = [
        [board[0][0], board[1][1], board[2][2]],
        [board[2][0], board[1][1], board[0][2]],
    ]

    x = rows
    x.extend(columns)
    x.extend(diagonals)

    # verify rows + columns + diagonals == 8
    assert len(x) == 8

    # determine if 'player' is a winner
    # check every row, column, and diagonal
    return any([i.count(player)==3 for i in x])
```

Chapter 16

Sorting

You can sort a list by either sorting it in-place or by creating a sorted copy of the original list

Sorting In Place

The sort() method sorts a list in place. The original order of the items is lost.

```
x = [3,2,1]
x.sort()
```

x now contains

```
[1,2,3]
```

Creating A Sorted Copy

You can use the sorted() function to create a sorted copy of the original list.

```
x = [3,2,1]
y = sorted(x)
```

Reverse Sort

Both the sort() method and the sorted() function take an optional *reverse* parameter. The list is sorted in reverse order if *reverse=True*.

Specifying A Sort Key

Normally, list items are sorted by comparing their values. This means numbers are sorted numerically and strings are sorted alphabetically. The optional key parameter let's you define your own comparison function. This lets you sort items by any attribute, either built-in or computed.

Here is a default string sort. Normally, upper case sort before lower case.

```
>>> x = ['a', 'b', 'C', 'd']
>>> sorted(x)
['C', 'a', 'b', 'd']
```

Here is a case insensitive sort. The strings are converted to lower case before being compared.

```
>>> sorted(x, key=string.lower)
['a', 'b', 'C', 'd']
```

IMPORTANT: the key values are only used internally by the sort function. They do not appear in the output.

Lambda Functions

Key functions are often written using lambda expressions. You can learn more about them at https://docs.python.org/2/tutorial/controlflow.html#lambda-expressions

Here is an example of sorting numbers by their absolute value. The key is defined with a lambda expression.

```
>>> x = [1, 2, -1, 0]
>>> sorted(x, key=lambda i:abs(i))
[0, 1, -1, 2]
```

Chapter 17

Adding Items To A List

New items can be added anywhere in a list – at the end, at the beginning, or in the middle.

Adding One Item To The End

The append() method adds a single item to the end of a list. If the item contains multiple values (like a list or a tuple) the whole item is added.

```
z = ['a','b']
x = [1,2,3]
x.append(99)
x.append(z)
```

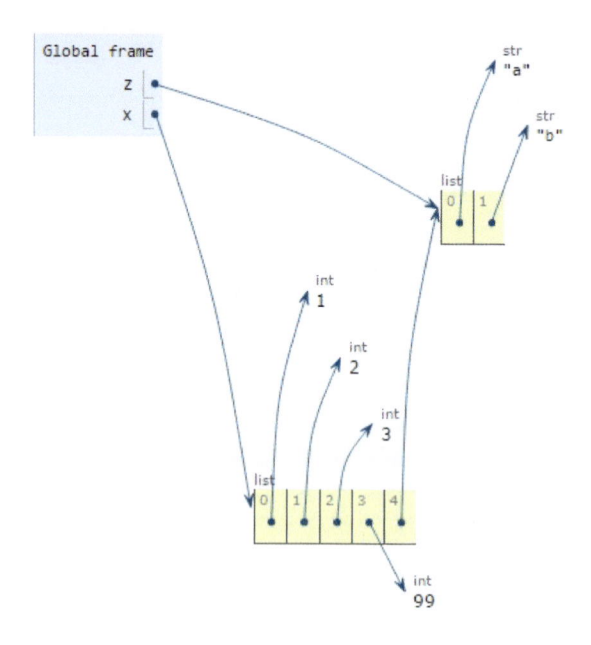

Notice how *x[4]* refers to the entire *z* list.

Extending A List

The extend method works by iterating over an object and appending the values one by one.

```
z = ['a','b']
x = [1,2,3]
x.append(99)
x.extend(z)
```

ADDING ONE ITEM IN THE MIDDLE

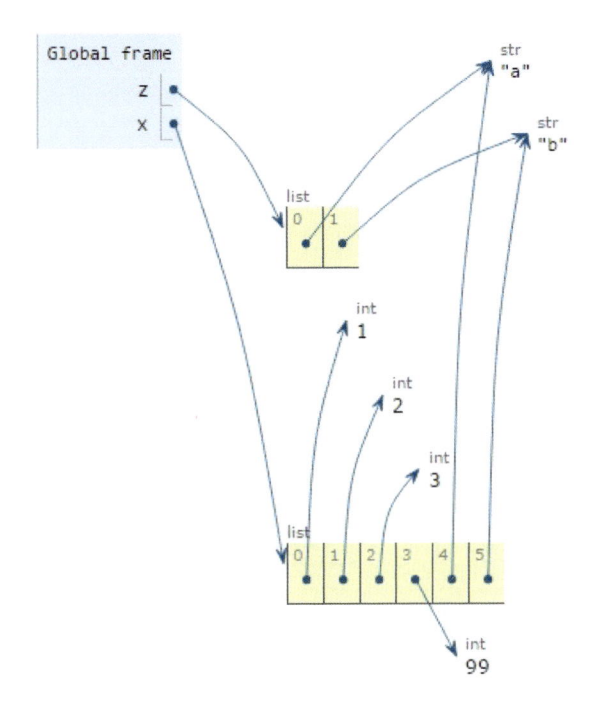

Compare this diagram to the previous one. Notice how the *z* list has been unpacked so that *x[4]* and *x[5]* now refer to "*a*" and "*b*".

NOTE: the parameter passed to extend() must be iterable.

Adding One Item In The Middle

The insert method will insert one new item ahead of an existing item.

```
x = [1,2,3]
index = 0
x.insert(index, 99)
```

x now contains *[99,1,2,3]*

Inserting into an empty list acts like append(). The index parameter is ignored.

```
>>> x = []
>>> x.insert(0, 'a')
>>> print(x)
'a'
```

Adding Multiple Items In The Middle

Slice assignment can be used to insert multiple values ahead of an existing item.

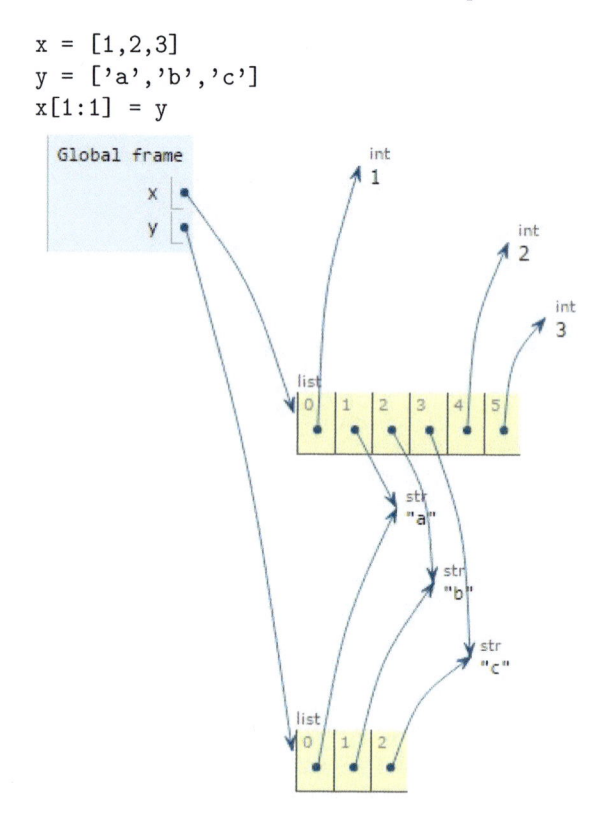

```
x = [1,2,3]
y = ['a','b','c']
x[1:1] = y
```

Chapter 18

Removing Items From a List

Removing An Item By Index

Use either the del statement

```
>>> x = ['a', 'b', 'c']
>>> del x[1]
>>> print(x)
['a', 'c']
```

or the pop() method

```
>>> x = ['a', 'b', 'c']
>>> x.pop(1)
>>> print(x)
['a', 'c']
```

if you know the index of the item you want to remove.
REMEMBER: del is a statement, not a function.

Removing One Or More Items By Value

The remove() method removes the first occurrence of an item from a list. Use a list comprehension filter if you want to remove all occurrences.

```
x = [1,2,3,2,1,2]
value_to_remove = 2
filtered_list = [value for value in x if value != value_to_remove]
```

will delete all occurrences of the number 2.

Chapter 19

Reversing a List

Reverse Method

The reverse() method performs an in-place reversal.

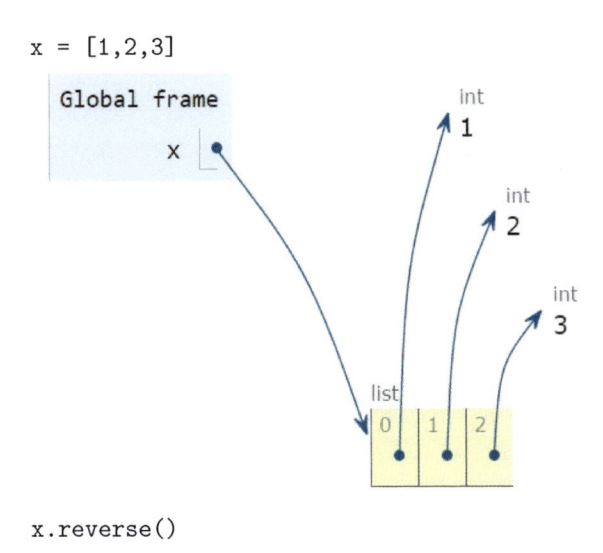

```
x = [1,2,3]
```

```
x.reverse()
```

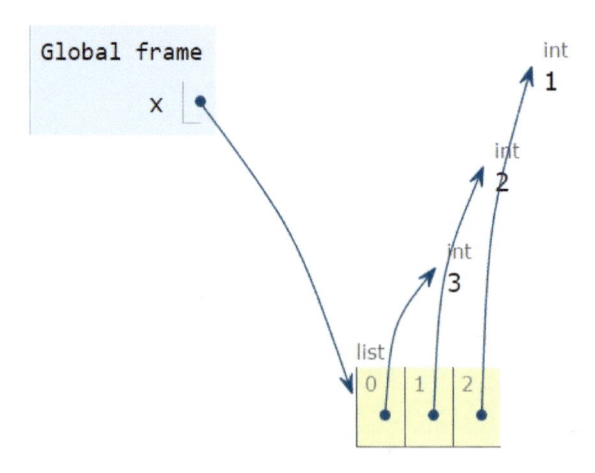

x now contains [3,2,1]

NOTE: the reverse() method modifies the original list. Use the reversed() function if you want to leave the original list unchanged.

Reversed Function

The reversed() function (spelled with a "d") returns an iterator object that will produce the items in reverse order. Use the list() function to create an actual list of values.

```
x = [1,2,3]
y = reversed(x)
y_list = list(y)
```

Chapter 20

Removing Duplicate Values

Removing Duplicates Without Preserving Order

You know that converting a list to a set will remove any duplicate values. You can use that fact to quickly remove duplicates if order is not important.

```
x = [1,2,1,2,3]
x = list(set(x))
```

Removing Duplicates While Preserving Order

There's no built-in function for doing this, but the code is not too hard to write. You just need to keep track of the values you've already seen.

```
x = [1,2,1,2,3,1]
not_seen = set(x)
unique_list = []
for value in x:
    if value in not_seen:         # is this a new value?
        unique_list.append(value) # add it to the output list
        not_seen.remove(value)    # remove it from the set
        if not not_seen:          # is the set empty?
            break
```

Chapter 21

Searching for Values

Testing For The Presence Of An Item

Use the *in* operator to test for the presence of an item.
 Given a list 'x'

    item *in* x

returns True if 'item' appears in x at least once.
 Or you can use the *count* method

    x.*count*(item)>0

NOTE: the 'in' operator is more efficient. It returns as soon as a match is found. The count method will always process the entire list.

Finding The Index Of An Item

Use the index() method if you need to know the position of an item.
 Given a list 'x'

    x.index(item)

returns the index of the *first occurrence* of the item. A ValueError exception is raised if x does not contain the item.

Finding The Indexes Of Duplicates

If 'item' appears in a list more than once and you need to know the index of *every* occurrence, use enumerate() with a list comprehension.

Given a list 'x'

```
indexes = [index for index, value in enumerate(x) if value == item]
```

Finding The Largest Or Smallest Value

Use the max() and min() functions to find the largest or smallest item in a list.

Finding The Index Of The Largest Or Smallest Value

The max() and min() functions take an optional key parameter. The key specifies the value to use when comparing objects.

To find the index of the largest item, first use enumerate to pair each item with its index. Then call max() and use the key to compare the values while ignoring the indexes.

```
pairs = enumerate(x)
index, value = max(pairs, key=lambda pair:pair[1])
```

You can write this in one line if you like.

```
index, value = max(enumerate(x), key=lambda pair:pair[1])
```

Chapter 22

Counting Values

Use len() to count the total number of items in a list. An empty list has a length of 0.

The Count() Method

Lists have a count() method. This method counts the total number of times a specified value appears in the list.

```
x = [1,2,3,1,2,1]
```

x.count(1) equals 3

The Counter Class

The count() method is not very efficient if you want to count every item in a list because you need to count the items individually.

```
x = [1,2,3,1,2,1]
counts = dict()
items = set(x)
for item in items:
    counts[item] = x.count(item)
```

In this situation the *collections.Counter* class is a better choice. The *Counter* object creates a dictionary containing an *{item:count}* entry for each item. The items can be used as dictionary keys to retrieve the counts.

```
from collections import Counter
x = ['a', 'b', 'a']
counter = Counter(x)
```

The variable counter now contains *'a':2, 'b':1* and *counter['a']* returns 2.

Counters are smarter than regular dictionaries. They can be added together to accumulate counts. Here the counts from y are added to the previous counts from x.

```
y = ['a', 'b', 'c', 'd']
counter += Counter(y)
```

Counters can also be used to analyze text. Given a string named 'text',

```
Counter(text.split())
```

will split the string into a list of words and count the number of times each word appears.

Index

\+ operator, 51
== *operator*, 47
__iter__() method, 19
__next__() method, 19
[ ] operator, 9

all() function, 48
any() function, 48
append() method, 59

chain() function, 51
collections.Counter class, 71
comma, 8
comprehension, 63, 70
concatenation of lists, 51
copy() function, 35
copying, with copy() function, 24
copying, with list() function, 24
count() method, 69, 71
Counter object, 71

del statement, 63
dict() function, 14
duplicate values, removing, 67

empty lists, 9
end, of slice, 29, 35, 40, 43
enumerate() function, 20, 70
extend() method, 60

for statement, 20
for statement, in comprehension, 45

if statement, 48

if statement, in comprehension, 45
in operator, 69
index() method, 69
insert() method, 61
is operator, 47
iterable, 19
iteration protocol, 19
iterator objects, 19
itertools, 51

key parameter, 70

lambda, 58, 70
list comprehension, 10, 45
list slice, forward, 39
list slice, reverse, 43
list slices, 35
list() function, 9, 35
list, last item of, 26
logical AND, 48
logical OR, 48

matrix columns, 53
matrix rows, 53
matrix transpose, 53
max() function, 70
min() function, 70

NameError exception, 46
negative subscripts, 25

pop() method, 63

range slices, 29

range() function, 27
remove() method, 63
repeat operator, 11
reverse sort, 57
reverse() method, 65
reversed copy, 36
reversed() function, 66

set() function, 13
sort key, 58
sort() method, 57
sorted() function, 57
split() method, 72
start, 27
start, of slice, 29, 35, 40, 43
step, 27
stop, 27
StopIteration exception, 19
stride, 29, 35, 40, 53

tic-tac-toe, 54
trailing comma, 8

unpacking, in a for statement, 21
unpacking, into function arguments, 17
unpacking, into variables, 15
unpacking, starred variable, 15
unzip() function, simulating, 53

ValueError exception, 69

while statement, 48

xrange() function, 27

zip() function, 51

Printed in Great Britain
by Amazon